Arwen The Dreamer
My Big Idea!

By Arwen & Marge Di Blasio

Illustrated by Ayan Mansoori | Formatted by Ell Om

ISBN: 978-1-7777509-6-1 (Paperback)

www.investmentforsuccess.com/books

For all curious minds,
we are born to create.

It was a rainy day and too wet to go outside to play. Arwen had a Big Idea. She thought of opening her own store. Her eyes sparkled like diamonds as she imagined what her store would be like.

"I can't wait to get started!" exclaimed Arwen.

FUN CREATIVITY DAY

She thought of having a pet shop, fashion store, toy store, and more. Endless possibilities that she could make.

She drew for an hour...

and another hour

...and another hour.

She worked throughout the day to create her big idea, but after looking at everything she'd done, she still felt something was missing.

"Will they even like it? What if they don't?" asked Arwen.

Arwen started to worry about everything. As she thought of all the possible things that could happen, she fell asleep. In her dream, she saw four blue doors. Wondering what was inside, Arwen knocked.

"Hellooooo... Helloooo... anybody there?" said Arwen.
But no one responded. She opened the first door
and said "Whoa!"

She saw a collection of fancy clothes, similar to what
she drew before she fell asleep.

"A fashion store!" said Arwen. Then a fairy came and
said "Glad you are visiting us today!"

Fashion Store

Arwen stared at the fairy and suddenly recognized her from one of her drawings.

"You're Anna! the fairy I drew!" exclaimed Arwen.

Anna the fairy smiled.

"Is this the place I built?" asked Arwen. She looked around and asked again, "Anna, is this for real?"

She couldn't believe that her idea had finally become a reality.

Anna nodded, and said, "You made something pretty awesome. See what you can do when you set your mind to it."

Anna passed a box to Arwen for her to keep.

Arwen opened the box and a word popped out!

"Decide?" asked Arwen.

"Remember, everything starts with a DECISION.
You can create whatever you wish," said Anna.

"I just have to decide," said Arwen.
"Thanks Anna fairy, I'll keep this in mind!"

Then Arwen headed over to the next door.

Arwen opened the second door and said "Whoa!"

She saw cats, dogs, birds, fishes, all the pets she
had imagined.

PET SHOP

Then a unicorn came and said
"I'm glad you're visiting us today."

Arwen couldn't talk for a moment.
She had seen the unicorn before.

Then she remembered the time she had
drawn a unicorn . She named her Uni.

"Uni, is that you?" asked Arwen.

Uni nodded and smiled. Arwen looked around
the petshop.

"You had an idea. You worked on it. This is the result
of what you created Arwen," said Uni.

Uni passed a box to Arwen for her to keep.
She opened the box and another word popped out.

"Believe?" she asked.

"Once you Decide, the next thing is to BELIEVE.
Believe that you can do it. Believe that you are doing it.
Believe, even when you don't see or feel it," explained Uni.

"Got it, thanks Uni," said Arwen.

Then she went over to the third door.

BELIEVE

Arwen opened the third door and said "Whoa!"

She saw stuffed animals, building blocks and dolls everywhere. "A toy store!" exclaimed Arwen.

Then a princess came and said "Glad you're visiting us today!"

Arwen stared at the princess. Like the fairy and the unicorn, she knew she had seen the princess before.

"Princess Charlotte is that you?" asked Arwen. She recognized her as one of the characters she drew when she worked on her big idea.

The princess nodded and smiled. "Look around and see what you have created Arwen," said the princess.

Princess Charlotte passed a box to Arwen for her to keep.

She opened the box and another word popped out.

"Action?" asked Arwen.

"Yes, your **ACTIONS** lead to results," said the princess.

"Decide, believe and then I have to take action to make things happen," whispered Arwen.

"Thanks Princess Charlotte," she said. Then Arwen went over to the last door.

She opened the last door, but this time,

she yelled "Whaaaa!" She couldn't believe what

she saw, it was another Arwen in the last room.

"You look exactly like me!" yelled Arwen.

"Yes, I'm you," said the other Arwen. "But, I'm the one that makes all the ideas come true. The one who finishes what you've started," she continued.

"What?" asked Arwen.

"You started working on your idea! You believed in yourself and took the first steps, but along the way, you got distracted. Then you stopped," said the other Arwen. "In the last box, you'll find what you need to finish what you started," she said.

She opened the box and a word popped out.

"Commit?" asked Arwen.

"Yes, you have to fully COMMIT until the end to make things come true. Take a small step every day," said the other Arwen.

DECIDE
BELIEVE
ACTION
COMMIT

"Decide, believe, take action and commit till the end," said Arwen.

"Decide, believe, take action and commit till the end," she said again.

Arwen kept thinking about these words and imagined herself finishing her big idea. Arwen felt good seeing what she could accomplish.

Finally, Arwen woke up. She focused on creating her fashion store, pet shop and toy store. She knew if she continued to believe in herself, take action and commit till the end, she could make it all come true.

And that's exactly what happened,

Arwen turned her big idea into reality.

PET SHOP
GRAND OPENING

Remember to commit
till the end.
Decide, Believe,
Take Action,
Commit till the end.

*2 Timothy 4:7 I have fought a good fight,
I have finished my course, I have kept the faith*

One More Thing...

Thanks again for reading our book.
We would love to hear what you think.

Could you please take a moment to review?

Your feedback can help others to learn more
about our book. It would also help
us understand how we can do better
and come up with more creative ideas
to share with you and others.

Many thanks,

Arwen and Mommy

Other Recommended Books

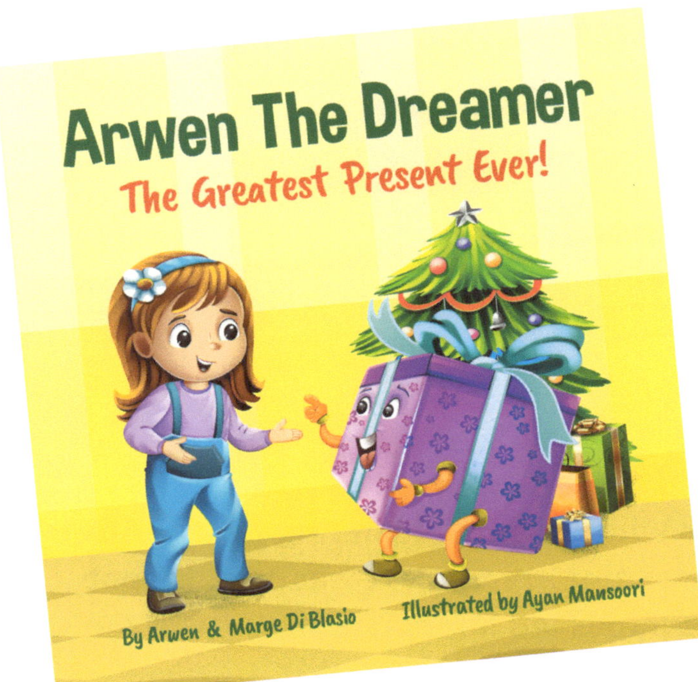

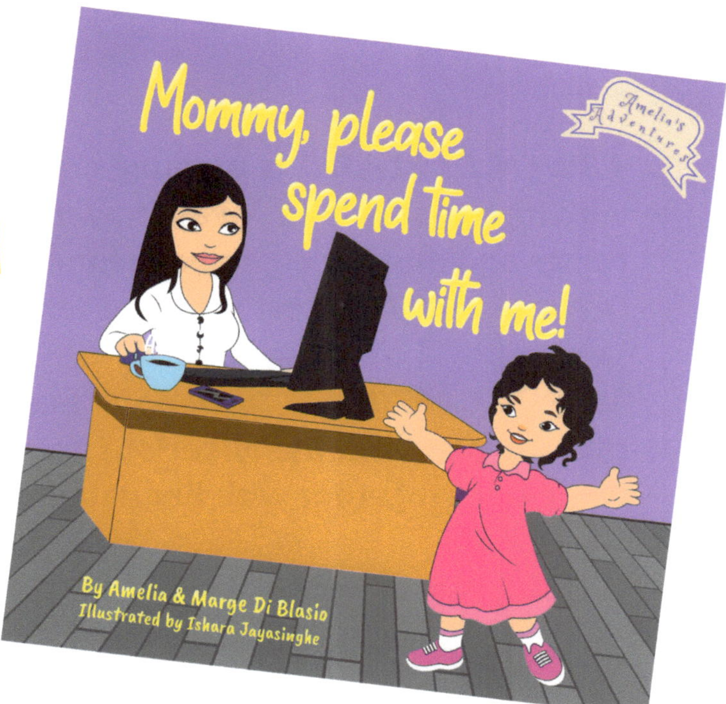

About the Authors

ARWEN DI BLASIO is a young creator who dreams of sharing her stories with the world. She loves drawing, painting, reading, creating different things and most of all, to have fun. She published her first book, *Arwen the Dreamer, The Greatest Present Ever* at the age of five years old.

MARGE CASTILLON DI BLASIO has published multiple books. She wrote this story for the many curious minds who wants to make their Big Idea come true, together with her daughter Arwen.

Connect with Marge and Arwen!

www.margediblasio.com